MOUSE AND COMPANY

MOUSE AND COMPANY

Story and Photographs by

LILO HESS

Charles Scribner's Sons · New York

A-2.72[MZ]

Printed in the United States of America
Library of Congress Catalog Card Number 76-37188
SBN 684-12810-1 (Trade cloth, RB)

MOUSE AND COMPANY

At dusk one day in the middle of summer a young female Deer Mouse left her mother's nest and protection to find a home of her own. This was not an easy matter, since the woods and bordering fields had many mice living there already.

A mouse is absolute ruler of its home territory as far as other mice are concerned. A territory has a network of roads, bridges, corridors, and crossings that are used daily by the mouse tenant to hurry and scurry over and under in its endless search for food. Each mouse has its own home or nest in a tree cavity, under a rock, in a fence row, in a hole in the ground, in a cluster of flowers, in buildings, or in empty birds' or squirrels' nests. Wherever there is a little seclusion and shelter, a mouse will make its home. An acre of land usually holds a population of eight to thirteen mice with their young, the latter leaving the territory when they are grown. The established mice fight off any mouse intruder, sometimes so severely that one opponent gets killed. Usually, however, the loser retreats with submissive squeaks, leaving the place for the victor.

A stable mouse population in an area does not seem to be connected with the availability of food and shelter, nor with the number of predators present. Scientists are now studying what really limits population growth or population explosion in mice.

An interesting experiment has been made with Voles (another name for Meadow Mice). Early in the year five males and eight females were isolated on one fenced acre. They were given high-quality food and good shelter, and there were no enemies present. The Vole population increased rapidly until there were forty-seven males and fifty-three females. Then, suddenly, something happened. The population declined. Females had smaller litters or none at all, and many individuals died. By fall the population had returned to the original number of animals: five males and eight females. No one is quite sure what causes such a change and we must wait for the results of further research to learn the answer.

The little female Deer Mouse needed to find shelter and home territory quickly and she continued her search. She was an attractive little creature, about two months old. She was about six inches long from the tip of her nose to the end of her long, tapering tail. Her fur was short and soft, light brown with white underparts and delicate white feet. She had expressive black eyes and long, sensitive whiskers which twitched and vibrated almost constantly.

The Deer Mouse and the White-Footed Mouse belong to a large group of mice called *Peromyscus,* which has many species and subspecies. The Deer Mouse probably gets its name because its color combination resembles that of the White-Tailed Deer; the White-Footed Mouse, because of its white feet. These two animals are so similar in appearance and behavior that only someone specialized in classifying animals according to natural relationship can tell them apart. The layman calls them by either name interchangeably.

Like all of its kind the young female Deer Mouse was a fast runner and a good jumper. She could jump almost seven times her own body length over the ground and about two to three feet high. From time to time she would interrupt her search for a home, glance around to make sure she was safe, and then, sitting on her haunches and steadying herself with her tail, wash and groom herself. For this she used her teeth, her tiny claws, and the pink palms of her front feet. Like a cat, she

washed her face; then turning, she combed her fur and finally her tail.

Suddenly she heard a rustling of leaves. For a second she stood motionless, listening and sniffing. Then, like a flash, she ran up a nearby pine tree and pressed close against a branch, remaining very still. Below, in the fading light, a white stripe stood out clearly, and its owner, a young skunk, came snuffling along. It stopped, pushed its nose under a rock to eat a snail, and then moved on.

When all was quiet again, the young Deer Mouse relaxed and started to investigate the pine tree. Running up and down its branches, she came upon an empty bird's nest. The nest was made of mud, twigs, grasses, and bits of roots and bark. It was very sturdy, and the dried pine needles that had fallen into it formed a nice lining. The female sat on the rim of the nest and watched and waited, probably to see if other mice, squirrels, or birds would chase her away.

When nothing happened she ran down the tree and investigated the immediate neighborhood. No one challenged her. She scurried over an area of about three thousand square feet; this would be her territory. Here she could probably find all the food and shelter she needed. As she ran along the boundaries of her new home, up branches and over rocks, she marked it with scent that was probably secreted through

glands on her feet and also with urine. Other mice smelling that marked area might cross the edges of the territory, but would not go near the center. "Scent marking" a territory is done by most mammals and is now being studied by scientists.

Wild mice are omnivorous, which means they eat animal as well as vegetable matter. In the summer they catch grasshoppers, beetles, and other insects for food, and they also eat berries, buds, fruits, and seeds. Occasionally they eat bits of meat from dead animals. In the fall they eat mostly nuts, corn, acorns, seeds, and grain, and they store large amounts of these foods in and near their nests for the winter.

The young Deer Mouse found some seeds to eat and nibbled wild strawberry blossoms. Then she washed herself again carefully and after that picked up some dry leaves and a few scraps of paper she found on the ground. She stuffed them into her cheek pouches and carried them back to the nest in the pine tree. She chewed the paper and leaves into fine shreds which made a soft bed for her new home.

During the following days the Deer Mouse made many collecting trips, bringing home more paper, dried grass, bits of moss, and even bird feathers and the downy hairs of dandelions. After all this material was chewed fine, it made a somewhat untidy-looking but good shelter.

One day a male Deer Mouse appeared and tried to share the nest with her. She fought his advances off for a little while, but he was persistent and so she let him stay with her. During the next few days they played together, chasing each other over stones and roots and through the tall weeds. They searched for food together and groomed each other's fur. One day they found a squirrel's nest in a hollow log. It was lined with leaves, paper, and pine needles, and stacked with acorns and various nuts. Since the squirrel was nowhere to be seen, the two Deer Mice moved in. They mated together, and a few days later the male left to mate with other Deer Mice.

The young female went back to the pine tree and reoccupied the old bird's nest. Twenty-one days after she had mated, her first litter was born—six babies, tiny pink creatures with wrinkled skin. Their heads were almost as large as their bodies and they could neither see nor hear. Their skin was so thin that when they had nursed, the milk could be seen in their stomachs. They wriggled and squirmed and made chirping sounds. The female was a devoted mother, and for the first two days she did not leave her babies, not even to eat or drink.

After the second day the babies began to show the beginning of the gray fur they were going to have. Each day the fine fur grew a little longer and thicker. When the mother

left the nest to search for food, some of the babies clung so tightly to her nipples that she dragged them along, down the tree trunk and over stones and branches. Sometimes a baby would fall off and the female had to carry it back into the nest. Grabbing it by the loose skin on the neck, or even by a leg, she half-carried, half-dragged it to safety.

After two weeks the babies' eyes opened, and they could also hear. They now had thick gray fur with white underparts, and they were very lively. Soon they ran and played in and outside the nest and started to eat seeds and berries. They were weaned when they were four weeks old and went with their mother everywhere.

This Deer Mouse family stayed in their bird's-nest home for the entire time the young were growing up. Other mouse mothers sometimes move their families to a different place if they feel that their nest has been discovered or disturbed. They frequently take the nesting material along from one nest to the other, like moving furniture.

When the little Deer Mice were two months old, they were as big as their mother. They had shed their gray baby fur and were the pretty light brown or tan color of the adults. They could take care of themselves and were ready to start a life of their own. Sometimes a few youngsters stay longer in the mother's territory or even in the old nest. The mother does

not usually drive them away, but makes a new clean nest for herself and the new family she will soon have.

Mice have several litters a year and there might be from two to nine young in one litter. An average litter consists of four to six babies. Probably no other mammal has as many enemies as the mouse. Only its high reproduction rate keeps it from becoming extinct. Raccoons, opossums, weasels, skunks, foxes, wolves, owls, hawks, and snakes are some of the animals that are continuously on the lookout for a mouse dinner. Only the fit, quick, and resourceful mice escape and survive.

In the winter the Deer Mouse often becomes a nuisance to man since it likes to make its winter home in buildings. It enters empty houses, cabins, lofts, cellars, or barns and constructs its nest in drawers, grain bins, upholstered chairs, mat-

tresses, and in any other place where it might feel sheltered, secluded, and warm. It chews on any kind of material, even wax candles and plaster walls. Any uncovered food is eaten.

Multitudes of mice and rats live in all parts of the world. The difference between the mouse and the rat is size. Between them they make up the largest mammal family, with hundreds of species and subspecies which scientists are still classifying, dividing, and regrouping.

Mice and rats are rodents, which makes them relatives of the porcupine, squirrel, guinea pig, agouti, beaver, and muskrat. All rodents are gnawers. Their two upper and two lower front teeth are large chisels which continue to grow throughout the animal's lifetime, and the rodent must gnaw to keep them filed down and in good shape. Some rodents are aquatic, others live in trees. Some even live underground, but most of them make their home on the surface. Desert, woods, mountains, swamps, and every other imaginable terrain provide homes for some kind of mouse or ratlike rodent.

Pack

The two main groups of mice and rats are the New World and Old World varieties. The underside of the New World mice and rats is usually a lighter color than their backs, while the Old World varieties are mostly uniform in color. These rodents are so closely related that they are just called mice or rats by the layman. To mention just a few of them: the hamsters with their large cheek pouches and short tails; the Asian Tree Mouse, which spends its life in trees and has a prehensile tail; the African Giant Rat, which might be three feet long; and the tiny European Harvest Mouse, which is only about three inches long.

Some have exaggerated long hind legs on which they can jump and hop in kangaroo fashion. One such animal is the Kangaroo Rat, which lives in desert country. Its family name is *Dipodomys,* which means "two-footed."

Some have stiff hairs and resemble tiny hedgehogs. These are mostly desert dwellers and are called Spiny Mice. Male and female Spiny Mice live amicably together in groups. They are often seen during the daytime, although they are actually nocturnal animals.

Several kinds of Wood Rats or, as they are usually called, Trader or Pack Rats, which come from North, Central, and parts of South America, often have lush, furry tails and very odd habits. They collect great masses of sticks, stones, and

Hamster

Kangaroo Rat

Spiny Mouse

bright shiny objects and bring them to their storage place. They take bits of glass, tin cans, and pieces of wire—even steal watches or jewelry if they find them—and in return they leave a worthless stone or stick, a habit that is not yet understood by man. One possible explanation is that they simply drop the object they are carrying when they find something that is shiny and more attractive to them.

An interesting mouselike creature which few people have actually seen, but of which almost everyone has heard, is the Dormouse. About forty different species of them are found in Europe, Asia, and Africa. Their name comes from the French word *dormir,* which means "to sleep." These little rodents store up a lot of fat during the summer, and with the first cold spell they crawl into a sheltered place, roll themselves into a ball with their tails curled over their heads, and fall into a deep sleep. They cannot easily be roused from this dormant state until the weather is warm again. Alice in Wonderland had trouble keeping the Dormouse awake when they attended the Mad Hatter's tea party.

Many species of Dormice are becoming extremely rare since hunting and insecticides have killed many of them. One species, the Fat or Edible Dormouse, *Glis glis,* was eaten as a delicacy by the old Romans, who dipped it in honey. Until they became scarce they were roasted and eaten in several coun-

tries, even in modern times. *Glis glis* is about the size of a chipmunk. It has soft gray fur, large, protruding eyes, and a long, bushy tail. Considering its size it eats enormous quantities of fruits and berries, nuts and seeds. It probably did great damage to orchards. It can be very aggressive, and if anything comes close to its nest, it is ready to attack with a loud chatter and sharp teeth. It becomes a pet only when raised from infancy. Most Dormice are now under close supervision and protection to preserve the species. Studies about their long, deep hibernating periods are now being made.

In biblical times the mouse was considered unclean. A reference in Leviticus 11:29 goes: "And these are unclean to you among the swarming things that swarm upon the earth: the weasel, the mouse, the great lizard according to its kind. . . ." The reference to the mouse might mean the Fat Dormouse, the Fat Sand Rat, or the Jerboa, all of which were supposedly eaten in former times. The Jerboa is a curious, long-legged, large-eared, mouselike creature which makes enormous leaps similar to those of the Kangaroo Rat.

Mice and rats are both friend and foe of man. Disney's Mickey Mouse is well loved, and the mice of fiction and poetry are usually portrayed as very appealing little creatures. The term "my little mouse" is sometimes an expression of endearment. Yet many people are repulsed by them and will climb up on chairs or tables when they see one. Scientists could probably not have discovered as much as they have about living things if it had not been for the mice and rats that were used in research and which are bred by the billions just for this purpose.

Since mice and rats can carry disease, soil food, and cause fires by gnawing through the electric wires, health departments, particularly of large congested cities, are greatly distressed by their presence. Over 15 million dollars are spent on rat and mouse control annually but make very little impact in reducing the population.

Farmers also hate them, not only for the grain and corn they actually eat, but because they make the other grain unusable for cattle feed by soiling it.

Many people, however, like them well enough to keep them as pets and to train them. No matter what the reaction to these small rodents is, they are an important part of the conservation picture. Mice and rats consume billions of weed seeds annually. Many seeds from trees, which they store in their hiding places but do not eat, grow and replenish our forests. Mice are also an important source of food for many predators that otherwise would eat more grouse, rabbits, or deer.

The mouse that is credited with most of the damage to man is the House Mouse, *Mus musculus.* It originated in Persia and probably spread first to Italy and Spain and then all over Europe and England. The House Mouse as well as the Common Brown or Norway Rat crossed the Atlantic as a stowaway on ships and was soon at home and established in the New World.

Although they are sometimes found in fields and marshes, they are most common in and near human habitats. Wherever garbage or food is left about, rats and mice can be found. They may make their homes in damp cellars, breezy attics, fancy

hotels or slum areas, in offices, stores, and even churches. The expression "poor as a church mouse" comes from the fact that there is very little food a mouse can eat in a church. Yet they somehow manage to survive even there. Their great adaptability and resourcefulness is the reason that they can survive in so many varied places. When poison is put out to destroy them, they soon develop genetic immunity to it, and they quickly learn to avoid traps.

The House Mouse, except for a musky odor that is usually unpleasant to humans, is really quite an attractive animal. It is from six to eight inches long, including the tail, which is sometimes longer than its body. It has short gray or brownish fur, but the ears and tail are furless.

The Greek naturalist Pliny credits mice with intuition and with the power to forecast events. He wrote: "When the collapse of a building is imminent, the mice migrate in advance." This could occur because mice and rats living in cellars might

hear the cracking of walls or feel drafts in a decaying building. Pliny also recommended mouse ashes mixed with honey to soothe an earache. An old Pennsylvania Dutch superstition claims mouse-pie as a cure for bed-wetting, measles, and whooping cough. In the Middle Ages, mice were thought to be made out of mud and to represent the ghost of a human soul. They were also believed to have been sent by God as a punishment to men.

The intelligence of mice and rats has been put to good use in laboratory studies dealing with the learning capability of animals. Mice and rats can learn to find their way through a maze with twenty-five blind alleys in just a few minutes. They also learn very quickly to press handles, bars, or levers and to solve innumerable similar experiments in order to obtain food pellets. Mice rank lower in intelligence than their cousin, the common rat.

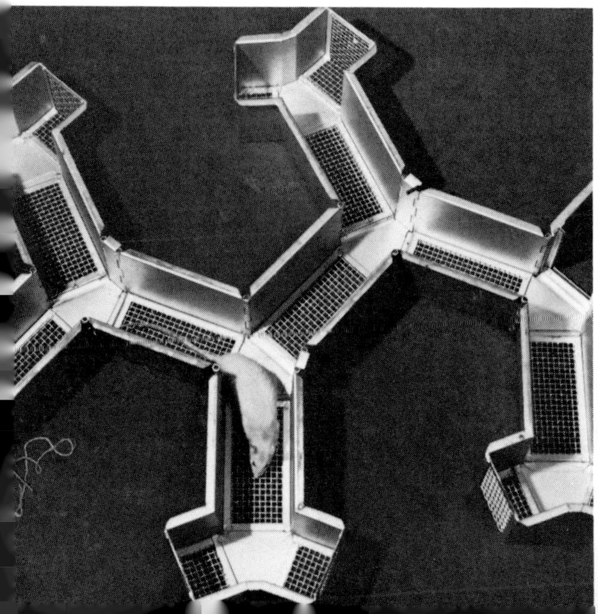

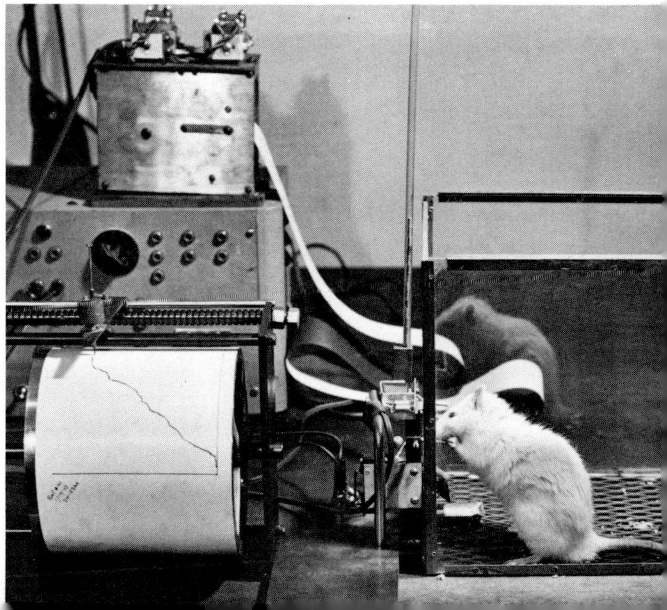

The House Mouse is the ancestor of all the so-called "fancy mice," and the Norway Rat is the forebearer of many types of cultured rats. By selecting and breeding albino individuals, a stable strain of white animals was obtained. Then, through crossbreeding various strains, the many varieties sold in pet stores and biological supply houses were obtained. More different kinds of mice are bred than rats. Almost any color combination can be obtained, ranging from black to gray, tan or reddish to white. There are also mice that are spotted, tailless, curly-tailed, long-haired, wavy-haired, and even hairless. When Hairless Mice are born, they have pink skin and no fur, but after a few days white fuzz appears and they soon become covered completely with white fur. After about four weeks they begin to shed their fur, starting at the head and neck, until they are hairless again, like their parents. The shedding process takes about a week to ten days.

Twist-Off

One popular pet that belongs to the larger family of mice is the Golden Hamster. Its native home is the desert of Syria and the Middle East. It lives in burrows about seven to eight feet underground. In 1938 a few were brought to this country as laboratory animals. About ten years later the hamster suddenly became a favorite pet, and many millions of them are raised and sold annually. Through selective breeding of mutants, many different colors and combinations of colors are now becoming popular. The name "hamster" means "hoarding" in German, and that is exactly what this little rodent does. It stuffs its cheek pouches so full of food that it looks as if it were afflicted with mumps. It then brings all its food to a storage place. In the wild such a storage place may hold fifty or sixty pounds of grain.

Another mouse cousin that has recently become a popular pet is the Mongolian Gerbil. In 1954 a group of twenty-two were imported to the United States, and all the gerbils in this country stem from that original little colony. In their native home in Asia they live in sandy and desert regions and their color matches that background. Like the hamster they dig tunnels underground, often on two levels, and they have large storage chambers. They are quite active by day. They eat roots, seeds, and some flesh. Other gerbil relatives are found in different parts of Asia and Africa. Most of them have

Hamster

Gerbil

long hind legs suitable for hopping kangaroo style. Their tails are haired and usually end in a tuft. If gerbils are handled gently when young, they make excellent pets.

One curious strain of mice that is sometimes found in pet stores is the Dancing or Waltzing Mouse. These mice look, eat, and breed like ordinary pet mice except that they have a strange deficiency in the middle ear which disturbs their sense of balance. They cannot move forward in a straight line but weave and wheel about in irregular loops and circles. This condition is hereditary. The path of the "waltzing" walk of these mice can be seen in the photograph. A bulb powered by a minute battery was attached to the back of the mouse. In a dark room a camera was set up with the lens wide open. The light on the mouse's back recorded the motion of the mouse on the film. At the end, a flashbulb exposure stopped the motion and showed the mouse with its powerpack. When Waltzing Mice walk backwards, however, their walk is almost normal. To demonstrate this, the mouse's maternal instincts were used. Some baby mice were removed from their nest box and placed a short distance away. The mother came out waltzing to retrieve them. She picked them up in her mouth and then, walking backwards, carried them in an almost straight line back to her nest.

Almost all mice and rats can be kept as pets. Although the domesticated ones are more placid and friendly than the wild ones, they can all bite and should be handled cautiously until well tamed. They can easily be kept in a classroom, nature

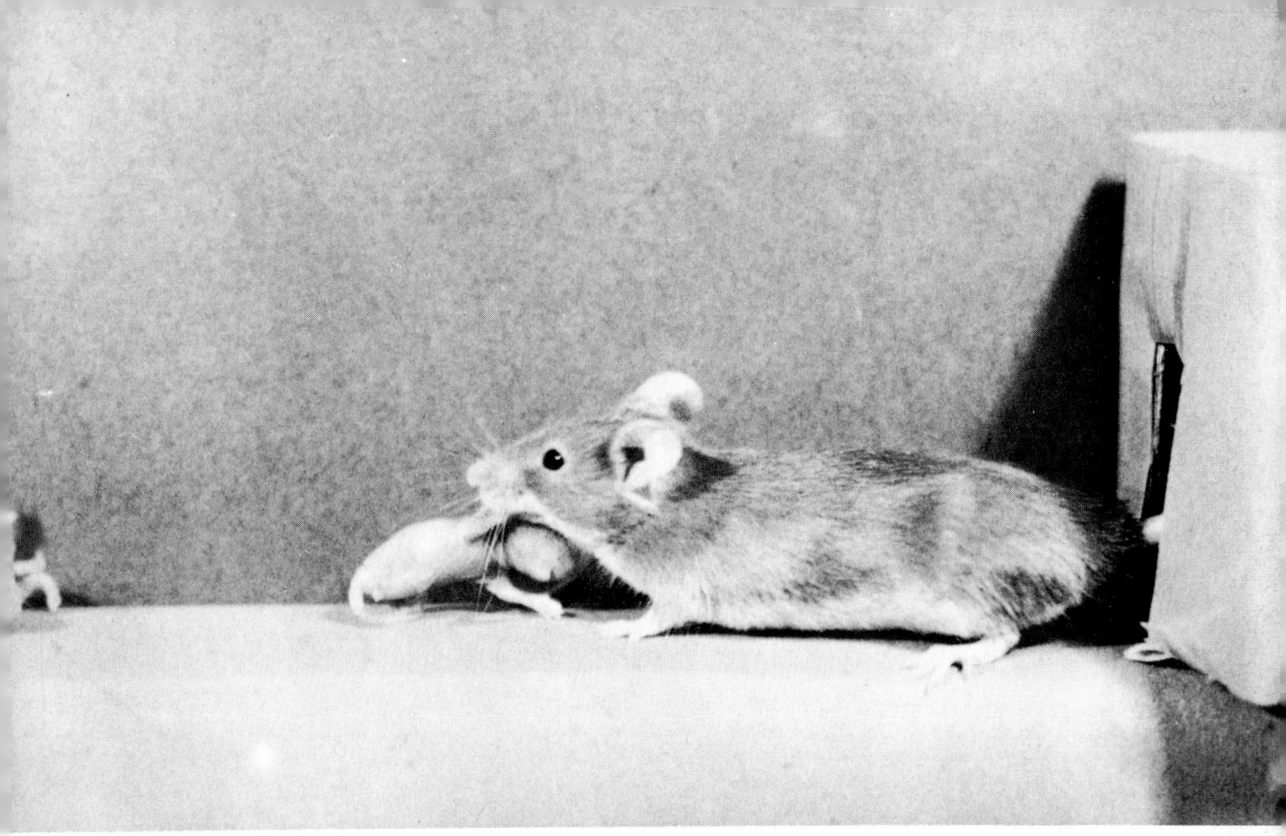

Waltzing Mouse

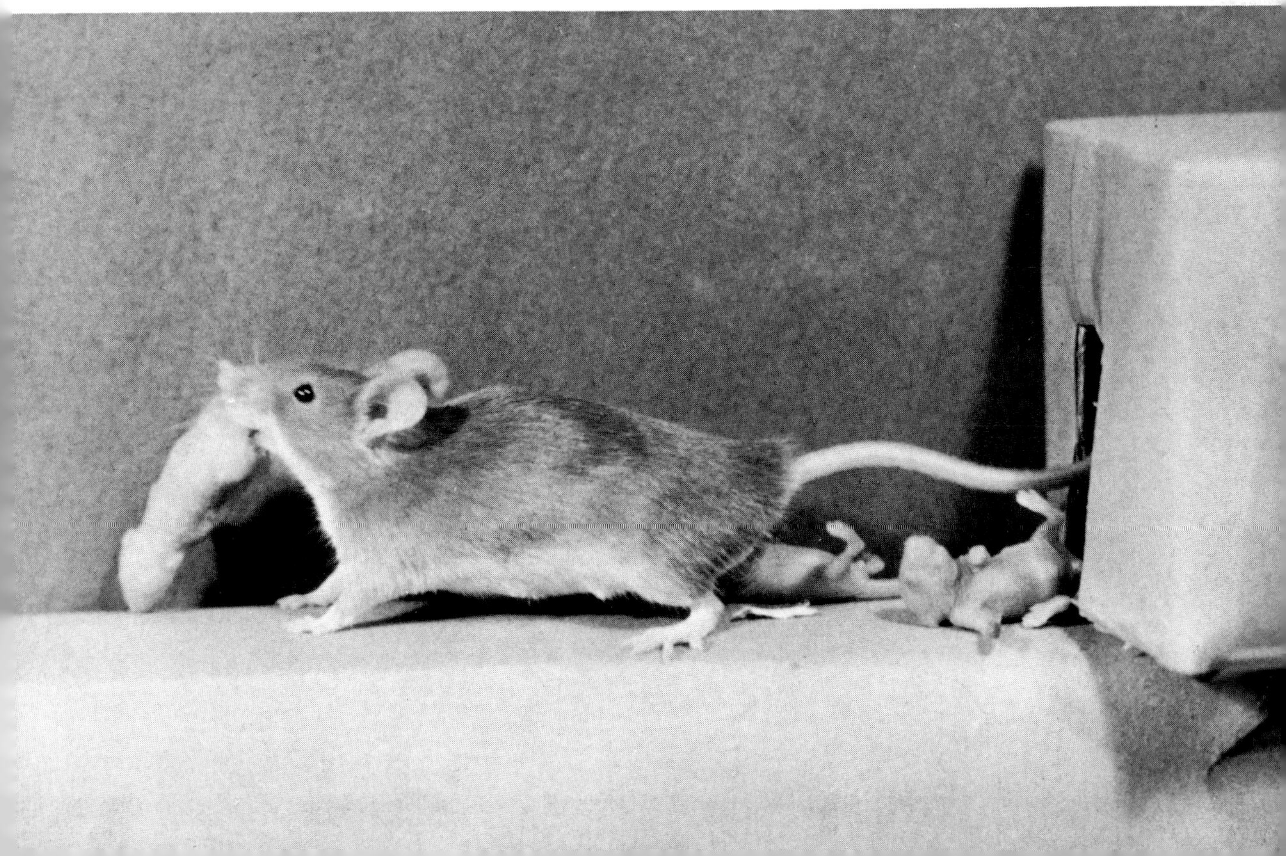

room, or at home since they require relatively small quarters, are easily cared for, and are clean. Not only are they interesting to observe and breed, but they can be used in simple experiments to demonstrate learning, behavior, and intelligence in animals.

A maze can easily be constructed by first drawing the pattern of it on a piece of cardboard or plywood, then setting strips of wood on the pattern between nails which have been driven into the board. The strips need not be more than two to four inches high. The maze must be covered with a sheet of glass or screening to keep the animals from climbing out. By counting and keeping records, many tests can be made. How long does it take a mouse or rat to find the food placed at the other end of the maze? How does a wild mouse compare to a domesticated one in learning? How many errors does each animal make? Do young mice learn quicker than older ones? After a few days the test should be repeated to see if and how long the animal can remember what it has learned. The same tests can be made with hamsters, gerbils, or guinea pigs.

Naturally all the animals must be well taken care of and kept clean. When school is closed for the weekend or the family leaves for a few days, the animals can be given enough food and water to survive. During vacation time arrangements must

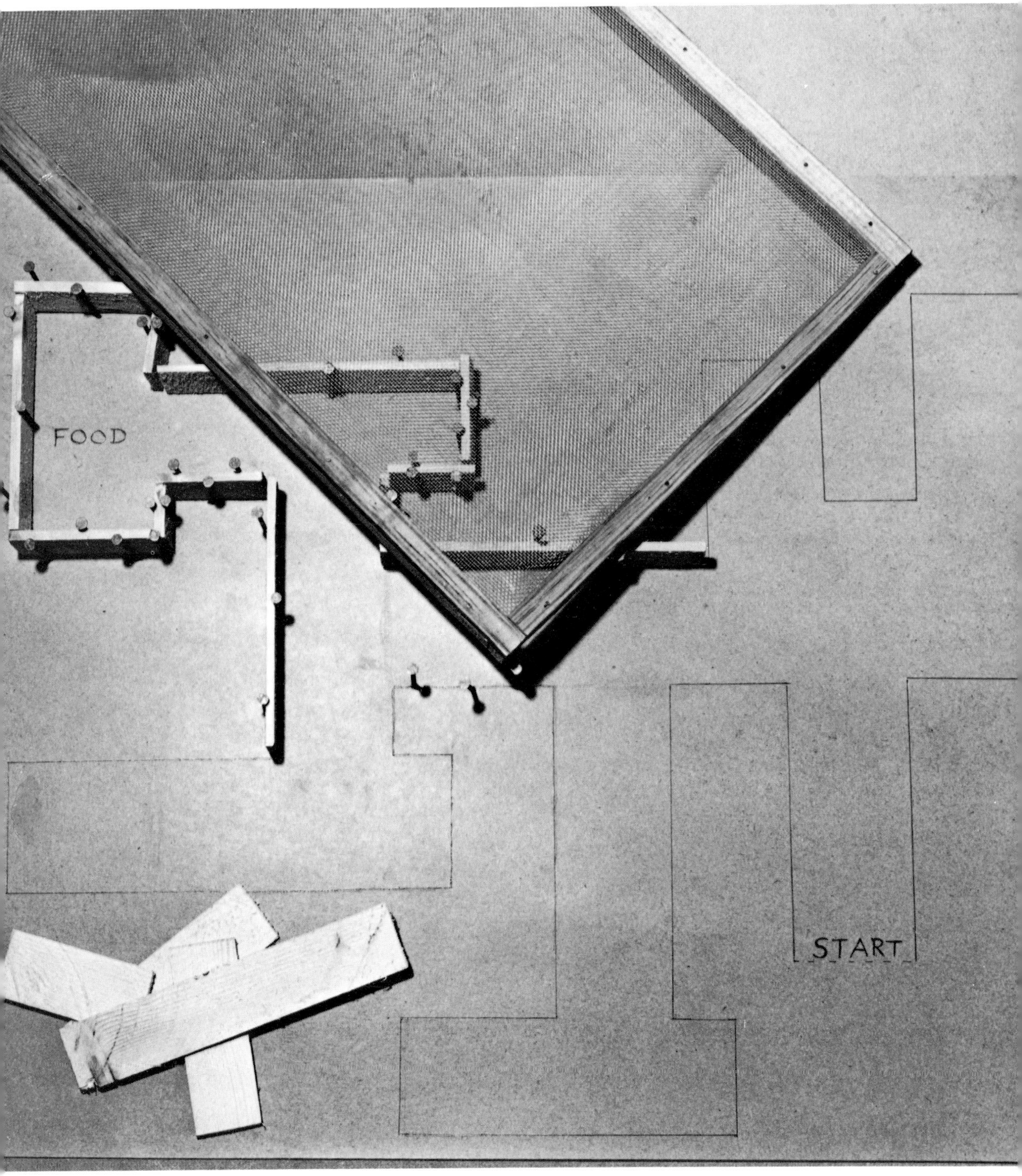
FOOD
START

be made with some dependable person to care for the animals, and wild animals that have been caught as adults can be released. Wild babies born in captivity usually will not know how to fend for themselves and must be cared for.

All these little rodents are good escape artists, and the wire mesh on their cages must be small enough so they cannot squeeze through it and strong enough so they cannot chew a hole through it. The commercial cages that have exercise wheels make good homes if they are big enough to place a nest box inside. All mice and rats need some privacy and it is cruel to deprive them of a hiding place. An old terrarium or fish-tank with a screen or wire mesh top can be made into a very good home for almost all of these animals. The round bowls that mouse laboratory breeders use are not very desirable since they provide no hiding place or exercise wheels. A female with young is best kept separately. An old tin can with the top removed or a plastic flowerpot can be used as a nest box. Cut a small hole in the side, by the open end, and place the can or flowerpot open-end-down into the cage. The animal will use the little cut opening as a doorway. A few tissues, paper towels, or commercial wood shavings should be put into the cage for the animals to line their nest with. Only white paper should be used. A piece of wood or little twigs must be pro-

vided so that the rodents can gnaw and keep their teeth sharp.

Most mice and rats drink water, and this should be kept in their cage at all times. The best way to provide this is to install an animal water-drinking bottle, available in all pet stores. This way the water is kept clean, and each animal can use what it needs. The desert rodents drink very little water.

The commercial food which consists of seeds, grains, and pellets should be supplemented with some fresh vegetables or fruits. Individual tastes vary, but apples, lettuce, carrots, and grapes are usually eaten. Dog biscuits, chopped meat, or mealworms fed twice a week will satisfy their need for flesh and protein. Whole-wheat bread soaked in milk is a healthy treat that most mice and their relatives will enjoy.

To catch wild mice, a "live" trap baited with corn, bacon, sweet buns, or sunflower seeds should be placed in the tall weeds or on the edge of the woods. The trap must be checked daily and any animal that is not needed should be immediately released. Never touch a wild mouse without a glove since it might bite. It should be kept in a separate cage for a few days to make sure it is healthy. It might be necessary to dust it with flea or lice powder. A new mouse should never be put into the cage with one that is already established in its home. The established one will fight or even kill the new one. In order to avoid this problem, both mice should be put together at the same time in a cage that neither of them has occupied before. In this way they can get used to the new quarters together.

The family of mice is large and varied, and each kind has its own way of life and behavior pattern. Each has different needs and tastes, but they all make interesting friends and pets when they are treated with consideration and understanding.

A listing of mice and other rodent relatives discussed

African Giant Rat, 24
Asian Tree Mouse, 24
Common Brown Rat. *See* Norway Rat
Dancing Mouse. *See* Waltzing Mouse
Deer Mouse, 7, 9–21
Dormouse, 26–28
European Harvest Mouse, 24
Edible Dormouse. *See* Fat Dormouse
Fat Dormouse, 26–28, 29
Fat Sand Rat, 29
Glis glis. See Fat Dormouse
Golden Hamster, 36
Hairless Mouse, 34
House Mouse, 30–33, 34
Jerboa, 29
Kangaroo Rat, 24, 29
Meadow Mouse. *See* Voles
Mongolian Gerbil, 36
Mus musculus. See House Mouse
Norway Rat, 30, 34
Pack Rat. *See* Wood Rat
Spiny Mouse, 24
Trader Rat. *See* Wood Rat
Waltzing Mouse, 39
White-Footed Mouse, 10
Wood Rat, 24–26
Voles, 9